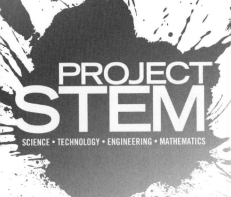

PROJECT STEM

SCIENCE • TECHNOLOGY • ENGINEERING • MATHEMATICS

Building
A Bug Box

Grades K–2

Glenview, Illinois • Boston, Massachusetts • Chandler, Arizona • Upper Saddle River, New Jersey

PEARSON

Teacher Reviewers

Candida M. Braun
West Fargo Public Schools
West Fargo, North Dakota

Sherri M. Gibson
Union Elementary STEM and
Demonstration School
Gallatin, Tennessee

Susan Holt
Union Elementary STEM and
Demonstration School
Gallatin, Tennessee

L. Jean Jackson
Old Mill Middle South
Annapolis, Maryland

Paul Keidel
Bismarck Public Schools
Bismarck, North Dakota

Martin Laine
Ayer-Shirley Middle School
Ayer, Massachusetts

Angelia Joy Long
Charles Carroll Middle School
New Carrollton, Maryland

Linda McShane
La Grange Public Schools District 102
La Grange Park, Illinois

Diana Mitchell
Union Elementary STEM and
Demonstration School
Gallatin, Tennessee

Bradd Smithson
John Glenn Middle School
Bedford, Massachusetts

Mary Reid Thompson
Union Elementary STEM and
Demonstration School
Gallatin, Tennessee

Leslie Yates
Union Elementary STEM and
Demonstration School
Gallatin, Tennessee

Acknowledgments

Photographs

Every effort has been made to secure permission and provide appropriate credit for photographic material. The publisher deeply regrets any omission and pledges to correct errors called to its attention in subsequent editions.

Unless otherwise acknowledged, all photographs are the property of Pearson Education, Inc.

Photo locators denoted as follows: Top (T), Center (C), Bottom (B), Left (L), Right (R), Background (Bkgd)

Building a Bug Box
Cover: (R) ©Incarnatus/Shutterstock, (C) ©jstan/Shutterstock, (CL) ©Tyler Fox/Shutterstock, (BC) ©Tasika/Shutterstock; **ivB** (BL) Jupiterimages/Thinkstock; **vB** (TR) Eric Raptosh/Glow Images; **viB** ©Mariusz Blach/Fotolia; **viiB** (CR) ©Fernando Blanco Calzada/Shutterstock; **viiiB** ©AlexGul/Shutterstock; **ixB** (TL) ©Anna Khomulo/Fotolia, (TR) ©Evgenly Ayupov/Shutterstock, (CR) ©thumb/Shutterstock; **xB** Photos to Go/Photolibrary.

Building a Greenhouse
Cover: (TL) ©Domen Colja/Fotolia, (TR) ©pio3/Shutterstock (C) ©Zarja/Shutterstock, (L) ©Nataliia Natykach/Shutterstock, (BR) ©blue67sign/Shutterstock; **ivG** (BL) Jupiterimages/Thinkstock; **vG** (TR) Eric Raptosh/Glow Images; **viG** ©Mariusz Blach/Fotolia; **viiG** (CR) ©Fernando Blanco Calzada/Shutterstock; **viiiG** (B) ©Henryk Sadura/Shutterstock; **ixG** (T) ©z03/ZUMA Press/NewsCom; **xG** ©Vitezslav Halamka/Fotolia.

PEARSON

ISBN-13:   978-0-13-319802-7
ISBN-10:   0-13-319802-2

8 16

Project STEM

Introduction to STEM

The Engineering Design Process . . . . ivB

What Is STEM? . . . . viB

Building a Bug Box

Introduction *Let's Look at Bugs* . . . . viiiB

Technology *High-Speed Camera* . . . . xB

Quick Lab *Where Are the Insects?* 1B

Vocabulary Practice. 3B

Math Practice *Time: Using a Calendar* 4B

Hands-on Inquiry *What Does a Cricket Need?*. 5B

STEM Project *Trap It and Learn!* 6B

Technology Zone *Insect Repellent* 16B

Career Spotlight *Optical Engineer* 18B

Enrichment *How Do Insects Get Food?* 20B

Assessment *Building a Bug Box* 22B

Performance Assessment *A Better Bug Box*. 24B

Test Prep 26B

Appendices

Safety Tips and Contract*

Making Measurements

Scientific Methods

*Review the Safety Tips and Contract before beginning each topic.

The Engineering Design Process

People use the engineering design process to make new things. Often they use the steps below. Sometimes they do the steps in a different order.

Find a Problem

Look for a problem.

Maybe something does not work well.

Maybe people need a new thing.

Choose a problem to work on.

Plan and Draw

Plan how to solve the problem.

Draw things you can make to solve your problem.

Your drawings are called designs.

Can you make the designs better?

Which design is the most useful?

Choose the design you think will work best.

Choose Materials

Choose materials.

Think about your materials.

Think of different ways to use them.

Then pick materials to make your design.

Make and Test

Make your design.

What you make is called a model.

Test your model to see if it works.

Test it many times.

What needs to be changed?

Most models need some changes.

Record and Share

Record your results.

Tell what worked and what did not work.

Think of other ways you could solve the problem next time.

What Is STEM?

Do engineers use science?

Do scientists use math? Of course they do!

Science, Technology, Engineering, and Math share lots of ideas and information.

Science

Science is a way of learning about the world around you.

Scientists observe nature.

They ask questions and do tests to find out about nature.

Technology

Technology is everywhere.

It is not just computers and TVs.

Your pen is technology.

So is your shoe.

Technology is using science to help solve problems.

STEM

Engineering

Engineering is using science to solve real-world problems.

Engineers find ways to meet our needs.

You can use engineering to solve problems too.

Math

Math is useful.

It can help you understand your data.

People use math to solve problems in science, technology, and engineering.

Let's Look at Bugs

They crawl on the ground.
They zoom through the air. What are they? BUGS!

Sometimes we use *bug* for the word for *insect*.
Insects are animals.
They have six legs. They are very small.
Why are they small? They do not have bones.
A thin shell covers a bug's body.
That is all it has to hold it up.

Some insects bug us. We call them pests.
But insects help us in many ways.
Bugs help plants grow.
They eat garbage. They move soil.
They move pollen from plant to plant.
They even help turn garbage into soil.

A hand lens makes it easy to see the parts of this butterfly.

A hand lens makes it easy to see the parts of this fly.

Try This!

Look at the insects on this page.
Talk about the parts you see.
Now look at another insect.
Draw what you see.
Look with a lens to see it larger.
Draw what you see.

Like all insects, ants have six legs.

High-Speed Camera

Some bugs fly. Some bugs jump.
Bugs can move very fast.
People who study bugs must be able to see them.

A high-speed camera takes pictures very fast.
Some take more than 1,000 pictures in one second!
People can take clear pictures of bugs as they fly.
It is like stopping time.

With these pictures, scientists learn how bugs move.
They can use what they learn to make things.
They can make robots that move like bugs.

This picture of a soldier beetle
is from a high-speed camera.
Otherwise the wings in the
picture would be a blur!

Try This!

Get a partner. Use a stopwatch.
How many times can you jump in 10 seconds?
How many times can you flap your arms?
Write your times. Take turns.
If you took a picture of the action,
would it be clear or blurry?

Name _____ Date _____

Quick Lab Where Are the Insects?

A **habitat** is where plants and animals live.
You find insects in all kinds of habitats.

Materials

☐ map
☐ pencil
☐ lens

1. Choose an area at your school.
Use the map your teacher gives you.

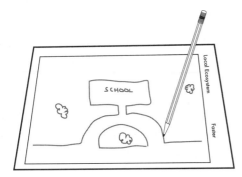

2. Choose an insect to study.
Mark on your map where the insect lives.

3. Observe. Use your hand lens.
Write four words to describe your insect.

_____   _____

_ _ _ _ _ _ _ _ _ _ _ _ _ _ _ _   _ _ _ _ _ _ _ _ _ _ _ _ _ _ _ _

_____   _____

_____   _____

_ _ _ _ _ _ _ _ _ _ _ _ _ _ _ _   _ _ _ _ _ _ _ _ _ _ _ _ _ _ _ _

_____   _____

4. Draw your insect and its habitat.
Use the space on the next page.

Building a Bug Box

Building a Bug Box

Name _____ Date _____

Vocabulary Practice

Draw a picture or write a definition for each word.
Use your science book or a dictionary to help.

Word	What it means
insect	
habitat	
adaptation	
lens	
data	

Building a Bug Box

Name _____   Date _____

Math Practice Time: Using a Calendar

Day of the week	Sunday	Monday	Tuesday	Wednesday	Thursday	Friday	Saturday
Number of insects		1	2	5	7	7	

There are 7 days in a week.

1. How many days of the week do you go to school?

   Ⓐ 1   Ⓑ 3   Ⓒ 5   Ⓓ 7

2. How many days of the week do you not go to school?

   Ⓐ 1   Ⓑ 2   Ⓒ 4   Ⓓ 6

Use the calendar to answer the questions.

3. Carlos sets his trap out on Monday.
On the third day there are 5 ants in the trap.
Which day of the week is it?

_____

- -

_____

4. Which days did he see the most insects?

_____

- -

_____

4B
Building a Bug Box

Name _____ Date _____

Hands-on Inquiry What Does a Cricket Need?

1. Observe the cricket each day.

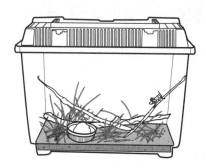

Materials

☐ cricket in habitat

2. What did the cricket do? Record what you saw with an X.

Cricket Observations				
Day	**Eats**	**Drinks**	**Moves Around**	**Rests**
1				
2				
3				
4				

Explain Your Results

3. Tell what the cricket needs. Use your observations.

_____

_____

_____

_____

5B

Building a Bug Box

Name _____ Date _____

Trap It and Learn!

Have you ever tried to watch a butterfly or a beetle?
Bugs can be hard to see. Many insects fly away.
Others may hide in dirt or leaves.

Scientists use traps to catch and study insects.
A bug trap must catch an insect without hurting it.
You will design and build a trap to catch an insect.
Start by asking yourself a few questions.

Find out where insects live.

Find out what insects eat.

Write what you discover here.

_____

- -

_____

_____

- -

_____

_____

- -

Building a Bug Box

Find a Problem

☑ **1.** What problem do you need to solve?

_____

- -

_____
_____

- -

_____
_____

- -

_____

☑ **2.** Where can you catch an insect?
Draw a picture that shows the place.

Building a Bug Box

Name _____ Date _____

Plan and Draw

☑ **3.** Look at the pictures of insects. How do insects move?

_____

- -

_____

- -

☑ **4.** Where can you find insects?
How can you attract insects?

_____

- -

_____

- -

☑ **5.** What could make your design difficult?

_____

- -

_____

- -

Building a Bug Box

☑ **6.** Use what you know to plan your trap.

Think about the insect you will trap.

- How does it move?

- What does it eat?

- Where does it live?

Draw a picture of the trap you will make.

Building a Bug Box

Name _____ Date _____

Choose Materials

Look at the materials your teacher gives you.
Think about how to use the materials to make the trap.

☑ **7.** What materials will you use to make your trap?
Explain why.

_____

- -

_____

_____

- -

_____

_____

- -

_____

_____

- -

_____

☑ **8.** Pick one material you did not choose.
Tell why you will not use that material.

_____

- -

_____

_____

- -

_____

_____

- -

_____

10B
Building a Bug Box

☑ **9.** Think about the materials you will use.
Do the materials give you new ideas for your design?
Draw what your trap will look like.
Label the materials in your drawing.

STEM Project

Name _____ Date _____

Make and Test

Build your insect trap.

Go outside and test your trap.

☑ **10.** Draw your trap as it looks outside.
Label all the parts.

Building a Bug Box

☑ **11.** Leave your trap for at least one hour.
Return and observe your trap.
Draw what you see.

☑ **12.** Check your trap once a day for five days.
Record the number of insects in the trap.
Tell what the insects are doing.

Day of the week					
Number of insects					

_____

- -

_____

- -

Building a Bug Box

Name _____ Date _____

Record and Share

☑ **13.** Did your design work? Explain.

_____
- -
_____
- -
_____
- -
_____

☑ **14.** Compare your trap with another trap.
How are the traps alike?
How are the traps different?

_____
- -
_____
- -
_____
- -
_____
- -
_____

Building a Bug Box

☑ **15.** How can you change your trap to make it work better?
Draw and label the new design.
Tell how the changes would make your trap better.

Building a Bug Box

Technology Zone Insect Repellent

Technology is using science to help solve problems.

You know the world needs bugs.

You know some good things bugs do.

But it's no fun when a bug bites you!

People use technology to keep bugs away.

Things that keep bugs away are called **insect repellents.**

People found a plant that mosquitoes do not like.

The plant makes an oil called **citronella.**

You can rub lotion with citronella on your skin.

The mosquitoes stay away from you.

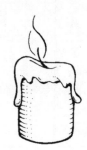

Citronella oil is also put in candles.

When the candle burns, the oil goes into the air.

The mosquitoes stay away.

Insect repellents can help keep bugs from biting you!

Building a Bug Box

Check Your Understanding

1. What problem about bugs did people need to solve?

_____

- -

_____

2. How did they solve the problem?

_____

- -

_____

- -

_____

3. How do people use technology to keep insects away?

_____

- -

_____

- -

_____

4. Insect repellents keep bugs away.
What are some other ways to keep bugs away?

_____

- -

_____

- -

_____

Building a Bug Box

Career Spotlight Optical Engineer

Optical engineers study the way light moves.

They observe the way light bounces off objects.

They make tools to help light bounce off objects they want to use.

Why might optical engineers study insects?

Light bounces off the body of one insect in a special way.

This helps hide the insect from other animals.

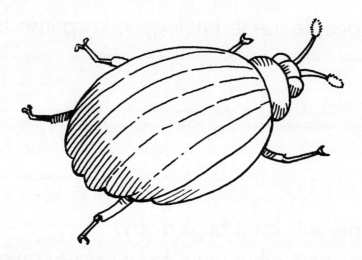

Optical engineers use what they learn.

They make new tools that light bounces off in the same way as it does off the insect.

This makes the objects harder to see.

Building a Bug Box

Check Your Understanding

1. What do optical engineers do?

_____

- -

_____

- -

_____

2. How do optical engineers use what they learn?

- -

_____

- -

_____

- -

_____

3. Use a hand lens to look at a real insect in class.
What colors is it? Is it shiny or dull?
Are there any parts the light bounces off in a special way?
Explain.

_____

- -

_____

- -

_____

19B
Building a Bug Box

Enrichment   How Do Insects Get Food?

Insects can get food in two ways.

Some insects drink their food.

Some insects chew their food.

Butterflies drink water and nectar for food.

Butterflies have a mouth part shaped like a tube. It is called a **proboscis.**

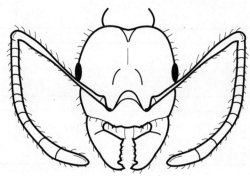

Ants chew their food.

Ants have jaws that can grab or cut called **mandibles.**

1. How is a proboscis like a mandible?

_____

- -

_____

2. How is a proboscis different from a mandible?

_____

- -

_____

- -

_____

Building a Bug Box

Name _____ Date _____

Notes

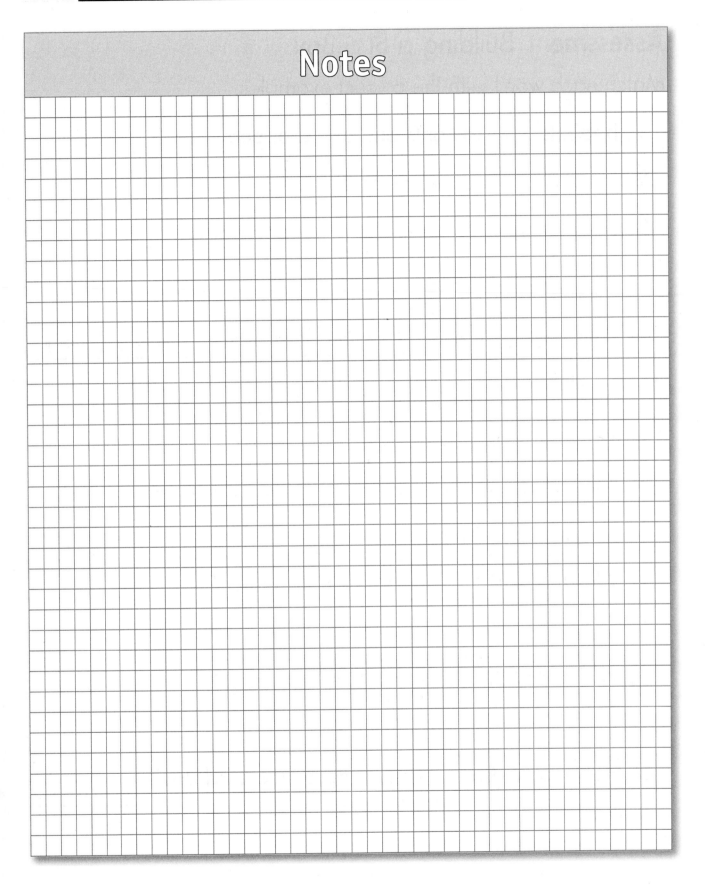

Building a Bug Box

Assessment Building a Bug Box

Match each word with the correct examples.

1. habitats   **a.** ants and grasshoppers

2. insects   **b.** wings and stingers

3. adaptations   **c.** forests, deserts, and parks

Use the calendar to answer the questions.

Day of the week	Monday	Tuesday	Wednesday	Thursday	Friday
Number of insects	4	3	7	2	8

4. Dora builds an insect trap.

She writes down the number of insects she traps.

She empties it every day.

Which day did Dora trap the most insects? _____

5. Which day did she trap the fewest insects? _____

6. How many insects did she trap on the third day? _____

Building a Bug Box

Name _____ Date _____

7. You are trying to trap an insect that likes sweet things.
The insect also likes to come out at night.
Design a trap for the insect. Draw the trap. Label the parts.

REVIEW THE BIG ? **What does an insect look like and how can you observe it better?**

8. You see a ladybug crawling on leaves of flowers.

You want to trap the ladybug.

Which is the best trap?

a. Put a piece of baked potato on the ground.

b. Hang some sugar water near a light.

c. Put an empty box under a plant that has flowers.

23B

Building a Bug Box

Performance Assessment A Better Bug Box

Some insects are small. Some insects are big.

Think about what makes a better bug trap.

Design the trap.

Think about how the new trap will be like the first trap.

Think about how the new trap will be different.

Design It

1. Redesign your insect trap.
   Draw a picture on the next page.

2. How is the new insect trap like your first design?

_____

- -

_____

- -

_____

3. How will you test your new design?

_____

- -

_____

- -

_____

Building a Bug Box

Name _____ Date _____

Notes

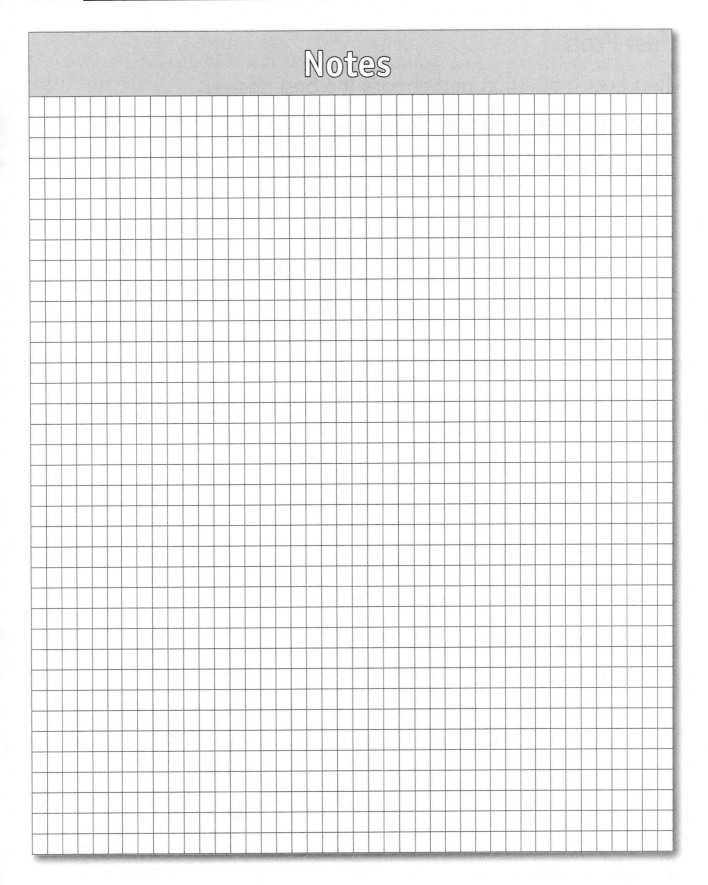

Building a Bug Box

Test Prep

Read each question and choose the best answer.

Then fill in the circle next to the correct answer.

1. What tool helps you see all parts of an insect?

(A) a telescope

(B) a thermometer

(C) a hand lens

(D) a greenhouse

2. June wants to build a bug trap. What should she do first?

(A) Draw a picture of the trap.

(B) Choose materials for the trap.

(C) Make and test the trap.

(D) Learn about the bugs she will trap.

3. Look at the picture.
Which animal would live in this habitat?

(A) butterfly

(B) goldfish

(C) ladybug

(D) worm

26B

Building a Bug Box

Name _____ Date _____

STEM GLOSSARY

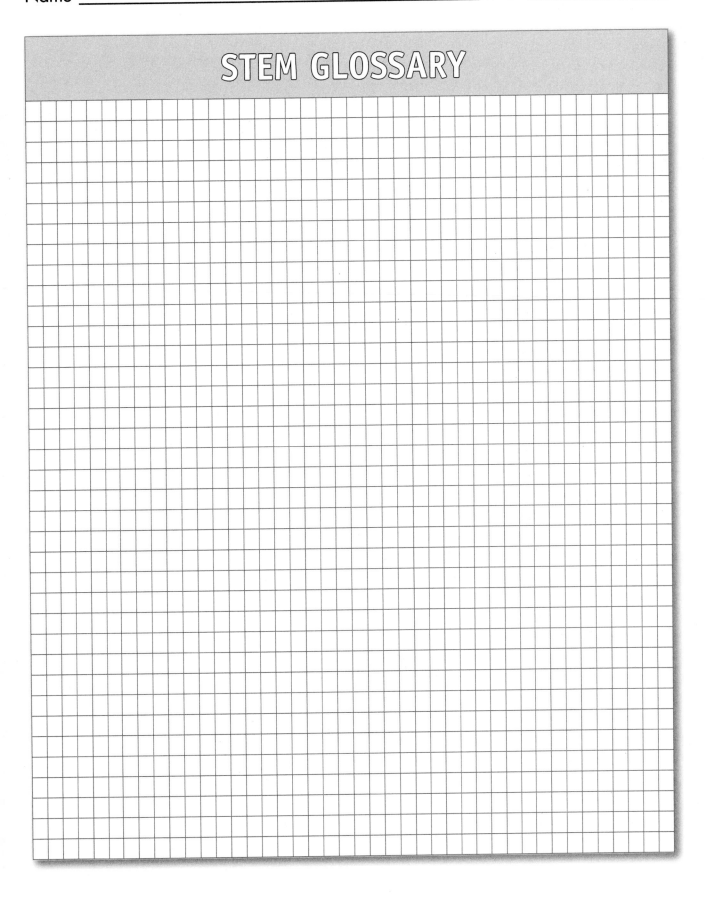

STEM GLOSSARY

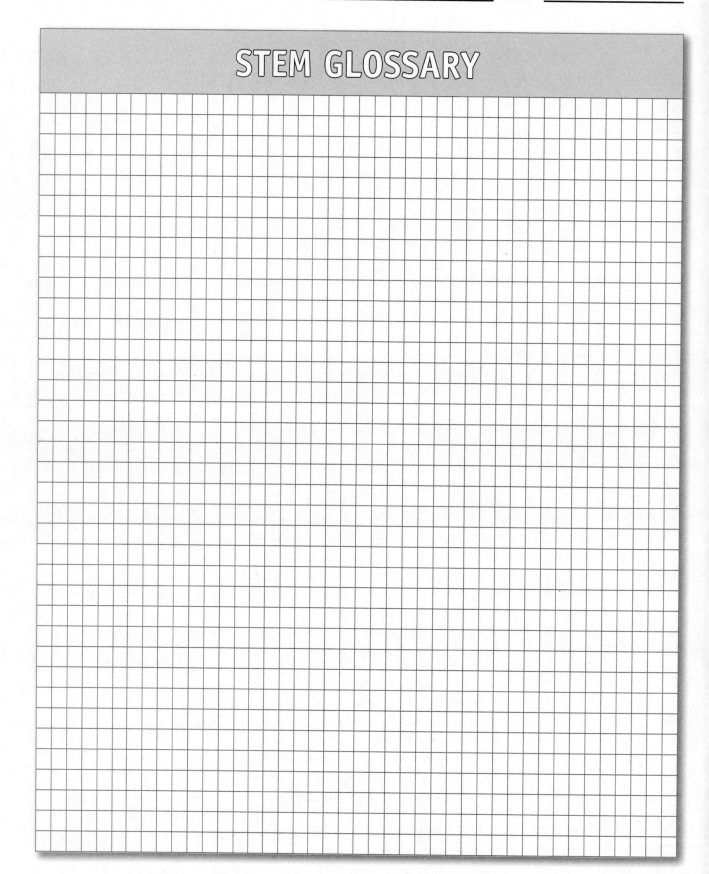

STEM GLOSSARY

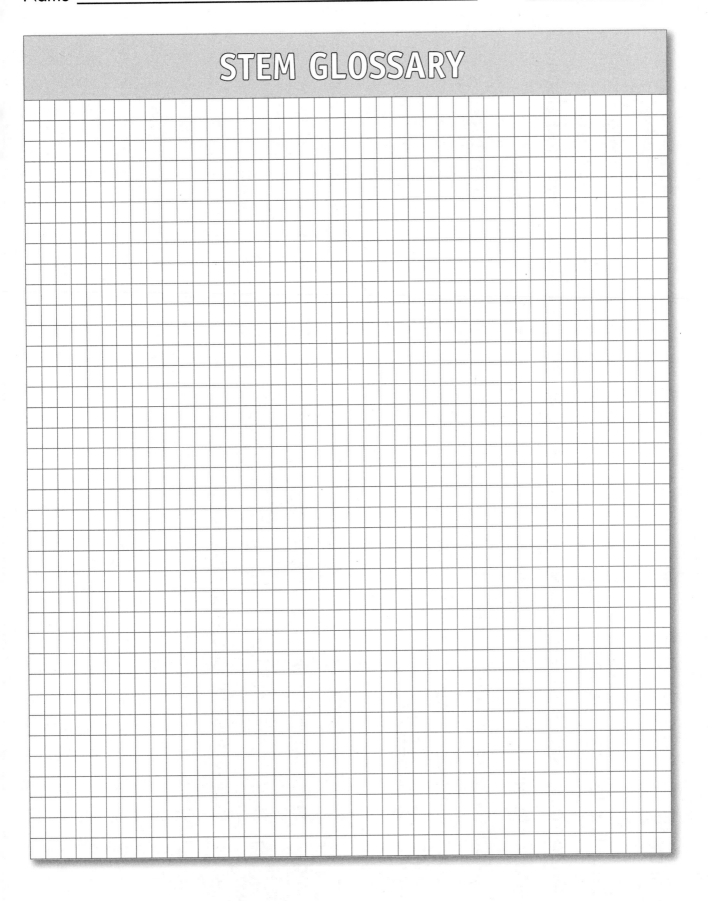

Lab Safety

Use these tips to stay safe in the lab.

- Listen to your teacher's instructions.
- Never taste or smell materials.
- Wear safety goggles when needed.
- Tie your hair back when needed.
- Handle tools carefully.

- Keep your workplace neat and clean.
- Clean up spills immediately.
- Wash your hands well after every activity.

Look for this stop sign in your book.

It warns you to be careful in the lab. Read the directions.

Follow the directions to stay safe.

Laboratory Safety Contract

I have read the Laboratory Safety Rules.
I understand the Laboratory Safety Rules.
I agree to follow the Laboratory Safety Rules.
I promise to:

(please check)

☑ Wear safety goggles.

☑ Listen to the teacher.

☑ Report accidents right away.

☑ Handle tools carefully.

☑ Keep my workplace clean.

☑ Clean up spills.

☑ Wash my hands after an activity.

_____

- - - - - - - - - - - - - - - - - - -

_____
(print full name)

Date - - - - - _____

Metric and Customary Measurements

Scientists use the metric system to measure things.
Metric measurement is used around the world.
Here is how different metric measurements
compare to customary measurements.

Volume

Liquid volume is measured in **liters (L)**.
Volume is the amount of space a liquid takes up.
One liter is greater than 4 cups.

Length

Length is measured in **meters (m)**.
Length is the distance between two points.
One meter is longer than 3 feet.

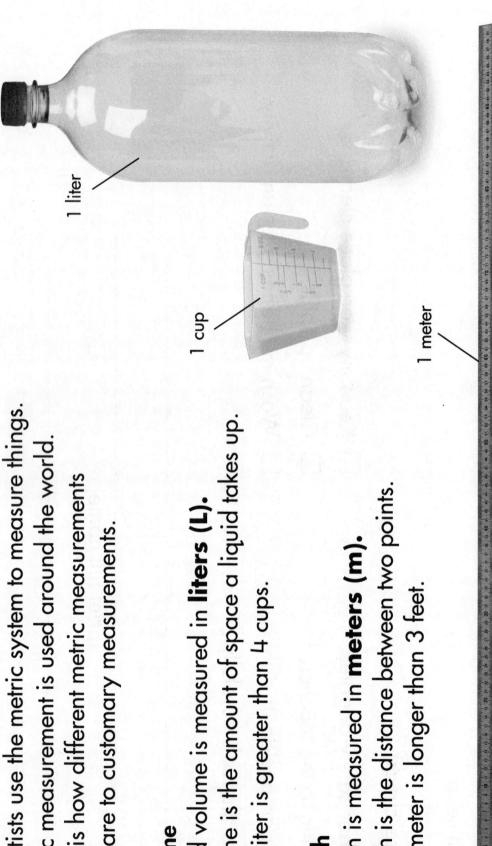

1 liter

1 cup

1 meter

1 foot

Mass

Mass is measured in **grams (g)** or **kilograms (kg)**.

Mass is the amount of matter in an object.

One gram is about the mass of a paper clip.

One kilogram is greater than 2 pounds.

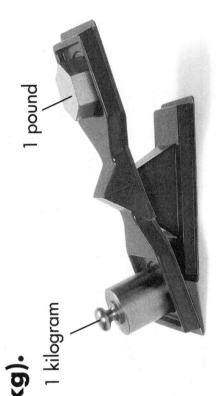

1 pound

1 kilogram

Temperature

Scientists use the **Celsius scale** to measure temperature.

Water freezes at 0°C, or 32°F.

Water boils at 100°C, or 212°F.

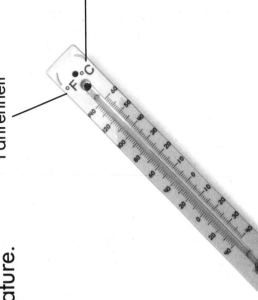

Fahrenheit

Celsius

Scientific Methods

Scientific methods are ways of finding answers.
Some scientists use scientific methods when they do experiments.
Scientists may not follow these steps in the same order each time.

Ask a question.

Ask a question that you want answered.

Make your hypothesis.

A hypothesis is a possible answer to your question.

Plan a fair test.

Change only one thing. Keep everything else the same.
Record your steps. Someone else should get the same answer
if they follow your steps.

Do your test.

Test your hypothesis. Repeat your test.
See if your results are the same.

Collect and record your data.

Keep records of what you observe.
Use words, numbers, or drawings to help.

Tell your conclusion.

Think about the results of your test.
Decide if your hypothesis is supported.
Tell what you decide.

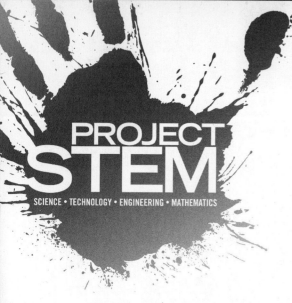

Building A Greenhouse

Grades K–2

Glenview, Illinois • Boston, Massachusetts • Chandler, Arizona • Upper Saddle River, New Jersey

PEARSON

Project STEM

Introduction to STEM

The Engineering Design Process . . . . ivG

What Is STEM? . . . . viG

Building a Greenhouse

Introduction *Warming Up with Greenhouses* . . . . viiiG

Career *Who Designs Greenhouses?* . . . . xG

Quick Lab *Which Is a Living Thing?* 1G

Vocabulary Practice. 2G

Math Practice *Measuring with Centimeters* 3G

Hands-on Inquiry *How Does a Seed Grow?* 4G

STEM Project *How Does a Greenhouse Work?* 5G

Technology Zone *Growing Crops on the Moon* 16G

Career Spotlight *Agricultural Engineer* 18G

Enrichment *What Is the Life Cycle of a Plant?* 20G

Assessment *Building a Greenhouse*. 21G

Performance Assessment *Building a Greenhouse Without Soil* 23G

Test Prep 25G

Appendices

Scientific Methods

Making Measurements

Safety Tips and Contract*

Review the Safety Tips and Contract before beginning each topic.

The Engineering Design Process

People use the engineering design process to make new things. Often they use the steps below. Sometimes they do the steps in a different order.

Find a Problem

Look for a problem.

Maybe something does not work well.

Maybe people need a new thing.

Choose a problem to work on.

Plan and Draw

Plan how to solve the problem.

Draw things you can make to solve your problem.

Your drawings are called designs.

Can you make the designs better?

Which design is the most useful?

Choose the design you think will work best.

Choose Materials

Choose materials.

Think about your materials.

Think of different ways to use them.

Then pick materials to make your design.

Make and Test

Make your design.

What you make is called a model.

Test your model to see if it works.

Test it many times.

What needs to be changed?

Most models need some changes.

Record and Share

Record your results.

Tell what worked and what did not work.

Think of other ways you could solve the problem next time.

What Is STEM?

Do engineers use science?

Do scientists use math? Of course they do!

Science, Technology, Engineering, and Math share lots of ideas and information.

Science

Science is a way of learning about the world around you.

Scientists observe nature.

They ask questions and do tests to find out about nature.

Technology

Technology is everywhere.

It is not just computers and TVs.

Your pen is technology.

So is your shoe.

Technology is using science to help solve problems.

STEM

Engineering

Engineering is using science to solve real-world problems.

Engineers find ways to meet our needs.

You can use engineering to solve problems too.

Math

Math is useful.

It can help you understand your data.

People use math to solve problems in science, technology, and engineering.

WARMING UP WITH GREENHOUSES

Do you think vegetables grow in cold snowy weather?
They can if they are in a greenhouse.
Plants inside a greenhouse grow even in cold weather.

Most greenhouses look like a glass shed or barn.
The glass lets light from the sun in.
The glass lets heat from the sun in, too.
The glass walls and roof trap the heat inside.

A greenhouse is hot and wet.
If it gets too hot, the plants might die.
A greenhouse must have a vent.
The vent lets hot air out.

Mitchell Park in Wisconsin

These glass domes are greenhouses.
Each dome has plants from around world.

Growing Plants at the South Pole

It stays a nice warm 70°F (21°C) or so in here.
The temperature outside stays below 0°F (−18°C).

Try This!

Draw a greenhouse on a piece of white paper.
Find or draw pictures of plants and flowers.
Cut out the pictures.
Group plants that are alike.
Glue the pictures down.

Who Designs Greenhouses?

Engineers make greenhouses.
They start with a plan or design.
The greenhouse must control heat.
It must control water.
It must control light.

A special greenhouse was built near the South Pole.
The plants there do not grow in soil.
They grow in water.
That greenhouse may lead to something amazing!
It may lead to a greenhouse on Mars!

What would a greenhouse on Mars look like?
Think about what plants need to grow.
How would you get those things for plants in space?

Try This!

Work with a partner.
Draw your design for a greenhouse on Mars.
Tell your partner how it works.

Name _____ Date _____

Quick Lab Which Is a Living Thing?

1. Put the seeds on the gravel.
Barely cover the gravel with water.

2. Record your observations.

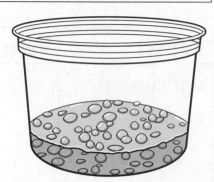

Daily Observations	
Day 1	
Day 2	
Day 3	
Day 4	
Day 5	

Explain Your Results

3. Which is a living thing? Explain how you know.

_____

- -

_____

- -

_____

Building a Greenhouse

Vocabulary Practice

Draw a picture or write a definition for each word.
Use your science book or a dictionary to help.

Word	What it means
agricultural engineer	
agriculture	
centimeter	
goal	
need	

Name _____ Date _____

Math Practice Measuring with Centimeters

A centimeter is a unit of length.
You can measure the length of objects.
A short way to write "centimeters" is "cm".

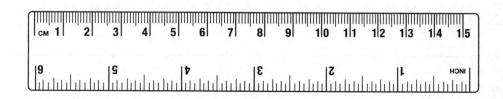

1. Measure one of your fingers.
Put your fingertip at the zero.
Then count the number of centimeters.

_____ cm

2. Measure your pencil. _____ cm

3. Measure a bean seed. _____ cm

Leaf A   Leaf B

4. Measure Leaf A. _____ cm

5. Measure Leaf B. _____ cm

Building a Greenhouse

Hands-on Inquiry How Does a Seed Grow?

1. Put the seeds and towel in a bag.
Seal. Put in a warm place.

2. Observe every other day.
Record your observations.

Materials
☐ 6 pinto bean seeds on a wet paper towel
☐ resealable plastic bag
☐ hand lens

Day 1	
Day 3	
Day 5	
Day 7	
Day 9	

Explain Your Results

3. Predict what will happen next.

_____

- -

_____

- -

Building a Greenhouse

How Does a Greenhouse Work?

A greenhouse is a building.

Most greenhouses have glass walls.

A greenhouse with glass walls lets
in sunlight.

Sunlight helps plants grow.

Plants can grow in a greenhouse.

You can build a greenhouse.

You will choose materials.

You will build your greenhouse.

You will grow a plant in your greenhouse.

Find how a greenhouse helps plants grow.

Find the best temperature for plants.
Discuss your ideas with a partner.

What needs to cover the greenhouse?
Write your answer here.

_____

- -

_____

Building a Greenhouse

Name _____ Date _____

Find a Problem

☑ **1.** You need a place to grow plants.
It is too cold to grow plants outside.
Write what you will build.

_____

- -

_____

☑ **2.** Draw what you will build.

Building a Greenhouse

Plan and Draw

☑ **3.** List the things a plant needs to help it grow.

_____

- -

_____

- -

_____

- -

_____

- -

_____

☑ **4.** How can a greenhouse help a plant grow?

_____

- -

_____

- -

_____

- -

_____

Building a Greenhouse

Name _____ Date _____

☑ **5.** Draw a bean seed.

Draw the bean seed after it grows into a plant.

Label the different parts of the bean plant.

Building a Greenhouse

Choose Materials

Look at the materials.
Think about how to make a greenhouse.

☑ **6.** Talk with a partner.
Discuss ways you might use the materials.

☑ **7.** What could make your design difficult?

_____
- -
_____
_____
- -
_____
_____
- -
_____

☑ **8.** Pick one material you will not use. Write why.

_____
- -
_____
_____
- -
_____

Building a Greenhouse

☑ **9.** Think about the materials you will use.
Do the materials give you new ideas for your design?
Draw what your greenhouse will look like.
Label the materials in your drawing.

Building a Greenhouse

Name _____ Date _____

Make and Test

☑ **10.** Build your greenhouse.

☑ **11.** Draw your greenhouse.
   Does your greenhouse look like a house? Explain.

_____

- -

_____

- -

_____

- -

11G
Building a Greenhouse

Name _____ Date _____

☑ **12.** Draw the plants in your greenhouse.
Measure the length of two leaves.
Do this on five different days.

Leaf Growth in Centimeters (cm)		
	Leaf A	**Leaf B**
Day 1		
Day 2		
Day 3		
Day 4		
Day 5		

Record and Share

☑ **13.** Compare your greenhouse with another greenhouse.
How are the greenhouses alike?

_____

- -

_____

_____

- -

_____

_____

- -

_____

☑ **14.** How are the greenhouses different?

_____

- -

_____

_____

- -

_____

_____

- -

_____

13G
Building a Greenhouse

Name _____ Date _____

☑ **15.** How will you change your plan?

_____
- -
_____
_____
- -
_____
_____
- -
_____

☑ **16.** Draw how your greenhouse will be different.

Building a Greenhouse

Name _____ Date _____

Notes Grid

Building a Greenhouse

Technology Zone Growing Crops on the Moon

Someday, people may live on the moon.
The moon has no soil or air.
How will people grow food?

Scientists have found ways to grow plants without soil.
They grow plants in special water.
The water has minerals that the plants need.
Growing plants in water instead of soil is called *hydroponics*.

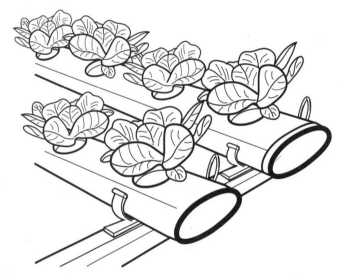

Astronauts may grow food on the moon using hydroponics.
They can make greenhouses on the moon.
They can grow plants in the greenhouses.
The greenhouses will be underground.
It will be safer for plants underground.
The greenhouses can give plants the water, air, and light they
need to grow.
This would give people on the moon food to eat.

16G

Building a Greenhouse

Design It

Design a greenhouse to use on the moon.
Draw a picture of it here.

Building a Greenhouse

Career Spotlight Agricultural Engineer

A hundred years ago, it took four farmers to
grow enough food for ten people.
Today, one farmer can grow enough food for 100 people.
Agricultural engineers have made it easier to grow food.

Agriculture is how we grow plants and raise animals.
Agricultural engineers use science to help farmers.
They help make plants stronger.
They find ways to grow more plants in places with less rain.
They make machines to help farmers.

Some agricultural engineers work in the fields.
Some work in labs.
Agricultural engineers find ways to grow more food with less.

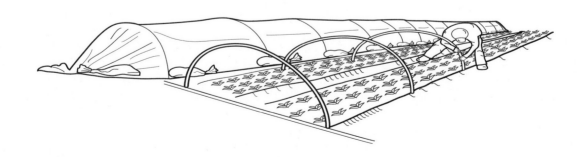

Building a Greenhouse

Design It

Redesign a tractor.

Include a feature that would help with crops and farming.

Tell how the new feature would help.

Building a Greenhouse

Name _____ Date _____

Enrichment What Is the Life Cycle of a Plant?

Plants need water to grow.
They also need air, sunlight, and the right
temperature.

1. The seed grows a stem and roots.

2. The pumpkin plant grows leaves.
   It can start making sugar for food.

3. Flowers start to form.
   The plant will soon grow a pumpkin.

4. The adult plant makes seeds inside the
   pumpkin.

1. What does a plant need to grow?

_____

- -

_____

2. What can a plant do when it grows leaves?

_____

- -

_____

Building a Greenhouse

Assessment Building a Greenhouse

Use the pictures to help answer the questions.

1. Label the different parts of the plant.

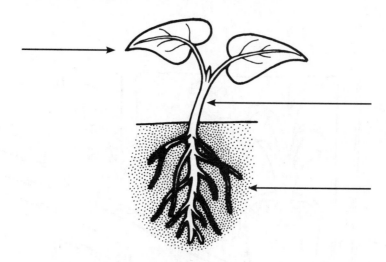

2. Tell how each part helps the plant.

_____

- -

_____

How can you grow plants when it is cold outside?

3. Lois builds a greenhouse in an area with a lot of sun.
What material would you use on the walls and roof?
Tell why you would use that material.

_____

- -

_____

- -

_____

21G

Building a Greenhouse

4. Juan is growing three plants.

He has a corn plant, an oak tree, and some violets.

Which plant has the right amount of space for its need?

Explain.

Building a Greenhouse

Performance Assessment
Building a Greenhouse Without Soil

Plants do not need soil to grow.

Plants need **nutrients** to grow.

Soil has nutrients in it.

Water helps move the nutrients from the soil to the plants.

All the plants need is water with nutrients in it.

Research ways plants are grown without soil.

Redesign your greenhouse so the plants can grow without using soil.

Design It

1. Draw a picture of what the new greenhouse will look like.

2. Make a way to test your new greenhouse.

Name _____ Date _____

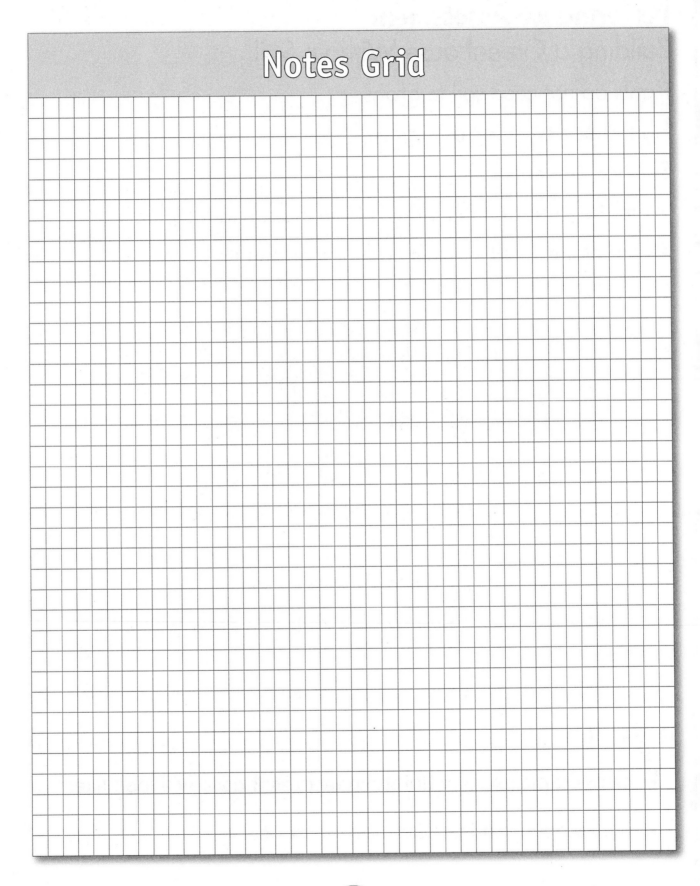

Notes Grid

Building a Greenhouse

Test Prep

Read each question and choose the best answer.

Then fill in the circle next to the correct answer.

1. What is something all plants need?

(**A**) water

(**B**) shade

(**C**) rest

(**D**) rocks

2. Look at the picture. Estimate.
How many centimeters long is the bug?

(**A**) 1 cm

(**B**) 3 cm

(**C**) 8 cm

(**D**) 13 cm

3. Working to grow plants is

(**A**) mathematics

(**B**) medicine

(**C**) history

(**D**) agriculture

25G

Building a Greenhouse